# MINDFULNESS? HOW TO KEEP YOUR MIND OUT OF STRESS AND ANXIETY

2

# Contents

3

## Understanding Mindfulness

The capacity to be completely present, cognizant of where we are located and what we are doing, and not unduly reactive or swamped by what is happening around us is known as mindfulness.

Every person has the ability to be mindful; you simply need to learn where to access it. It is not a trait that you have to summon.

Learning the definition of mindfulness and how it connects to meditation is a good place to start. Being mindful is the trait of being totally present and involved with whatever we are doing right now, without interruption or passing judgment, and conscious of our thoughts and emotions without becoming sucked into them. Through meditation, we practice this present-moment awareness, honing the ability of mindfulness that we may subsequently use in daily life. By training the mind to be present, we are also training ourselves to live more consciously – in the moment, breathing, and unattached to reactionary thoughts and emotions — which is especially useful when dealing with unpleasant situations or challenging circumstances.

Do you ever wonder how often a day you experience mindfulness? You may check where you stand by taking the Mindful Attention Awareness Score (MAAS), a 15-item quiz used by researchers to gauge mindfulness. The higher your score, the more adeptly you can practice mindfulness. You didn't get the grade you wanted. Not to worry! It's just a signal that you could benefit from practicing mindfulness meditation.

## The distinction between meditation and mindfulness

The issue about mindfulness that a lot of individuals find confounding is that it's not a passing mental state that appears during sitting and then disappears for the rest of the day. Instead, mindfulness is a way of life that, when we remember, enables us to take a step back and be in the present in any circumstance.

Although mindfulness doesn't make stress or other problems go away, it does give us more control over how we respond to them in the present, increasing our chances of responding in a composed and sympathetic manner when faced with stress or other difficulties. Of course, practicing mindfulness does not prevent us from experiencing anger; rather, it enables us to be more deliberate about how we want to react, whether that be with composure and empathy most of the time or, maybe, on occasion, with measured rage.

The practice of meditation is the foundation for developing awareness. We initially use meditation to spend a little amount of time becoming acquainted with the present moment.

But over time, daily mindfulness practice helps us hone the capacity to be present all day, every day.

**The best way to do mindfulness meditation**

In addition to changing our perspective and attitude, mindfulness meditation may also change the way our brains are wired. According to universal neuron imaging meditation research, eight weeks of meditation with mindfulness also affects our brains, changing them to prefer happier thoughts and feelings.

The first benefit of meditation is that it allows us to transition from high-voltage to lower-frequency brain waves, activation (and, perhaps more importantly, deactivating) certain brain areas. For example, it could reduce the strength of neuronal connections to the medial prefrontal cortex, or prefrontal cortex, sometimes known as the "me center," therefore lowering the presence of traits like stress, anxiety, and fear. The brain areas responsible for mental functions like focus and judgment may also develop new neural connections as a result of meditation.

And that's not all—mindfulness meditation may really change the structure of the brain according to a process known as neuron plasticity. According to study, consistent meditation practice causes the brain's gray matter, which affects feelings, planning, and problem-solving, as well as its cortex thickness, which controls memory and learning, to both increase. The amygdale, which governs how we perceive stress, fear, and anxiety, however, becomes smaller as we age.

## The Different Kinds of Meditation

Even while mindfulness is intrinsic, it may be developed using proven methods. Here are a few instances:

- Meditation while standing, sitting, or moving (laying down is also an option, however it often results in sleep);
- The little breaks we include in our daily activities;
- Combining meditation with other pursuits, including yoga or exercise.

It is possible to improve one's ability to think effectively over time. Since everything starts with the brain-heart connection, the more practice you have, the more intelligent you become. What do you think about re-establishing both connections?

**Here are some little-known techniques for thinking clearly. Let's investigate each secret one at a time.**

## Secret #1: Always consider the lesson you can learn from failure.

"It's okay to celebrate success, but it's more crucial to learn from failure" (Bill Gates)

Remember that the brain-heart link is where it all begins and ends. Therefore, if a terrible catastrophe occurs, try to learn something important from it. When you reflect on the situation, you view it as a lesson rather than as a terrible unfortunate event. Try to find fulfillment in everything. No matter whether it was a success or a loss, simply try to consider "What lesson you got from it?"

## 2.Your Mind's Response to Stress

The first step is to comprehend how your body and brain respond to stress naturally. Once you understand it, you may attempt to change your attitude toward stress by putting new strategies and ways of being into everyday practice. Our brains' neuroplasticity allows us to continuously practice and encounter new ways of thinking to change them.

Your brain's amygdale, an almond-shaped area, recognizes danger and sets off the stress response. Neurotransmitters and hormones like cortical, nor are epinephrine, and adrenaline just a few of those that are produced in reaction, getting your body ready for "fight or flight." If your brain feels you are unable to deal with the stressor, the sympathetic nervous system of the sympathetic nervous system may initiate a "freeze" response. Quickly follows the "fight, flight, or freeze" response. Your body may react to a snake on the road or an oncoming car before that you can even realize what you're facing.

## The third secret is to recognize your negative ideas and change them to positive ones.

"The right attitude can change a bad stress into a good stress," said Hans Sale.

Many individuals use self-defeating ideas like "I'm not good enough" and "I don't deserve this" to demotivate themselves, but this is never a smart idea. Everyone's prior experiences have an impact on them, and when we just focus negatively about them, that effect also shows up in the present. In order to change your negative ideas into good ones, constantly strive. To do that, all you need to do is adopt the proper mindset, and everything else will fall into place on its own.

## 4.Learn to slow your pace and relax

Before reacting to a stressful situation so that the prefrontal brain has time to register the response. This may be helpful for a variety of situations, including when a spouse or coworker criticizes you, when you discover an overdue bill, or while you are awaiting the results of a medical test.

## Secret #5: Constant thinking results in stagnation

Overanalyzing is the practice of inventing issues that did not exist.

Most individuals have the tendency of deliberating for too long even before making the slightest choice. Too much pondering, according to psychology, encourages inertia. Therefore, you should definitely avoid doing this and instead think like...

Create a thought for yourself.

Concept: Create a concept based on it.

Visualize the thought that enters your head.

Action: Go one step farther to put that thought into practice.

**6.Maintaining mindfulness is choosing to change your thoughts from irrational anxieties and fears to a welcoming, compassionate**

"Observer "position. You could question: "Hmm, what's going on here. My chest is starting to feel angry. I want to say something hurtful. Would doing it at this time be beneficial? The greatest way to practice mindfulness is to consistently meditate and to cultivate a thoughtful attitude when you are not under stress. According to brain research, while responding to an emotional stressor, persons who are more attentive have improved amygdale-prefrontal cortex connection.

**Secret #7: Recognize someone's intent before becoming hurt by their actions.**

'Don't judge the work by its cover,' they say.

The majority of individuals has short fuse and lose their patience easily. But you shouldn't be like them if you want to succeed in life. You must comprehend the motivation for the conduct before you are harmed. This will make asking for forgiveness more simpler and prevent you from being irritated or furious.

## 8. Find a Feeling of Control –

Research on rats, primates, and humans have shown that our bodies and brains react more negatively to unexpected, uncontrolled occurrences than to predictable, controllable ones. So consider the components of this circumstance that you can affect and those that you cannot, and concentrate your efforts on attempting to improve the aspects that you can (while working on accepting those you cannot with mindfulness).

## Secret #9: Powerful Thinking Is Triggered by Strong Words

"A word can alter meaning, emotion, and drive."

It is clear that strong language inspires strong thought. Let's assume that if you say, "I'll try this technique," the remark seems weak and too generic. However, when you say, "I must master this technique," it sounds strong and inspiring. Therefore, if you want to position yourself for success in your thoughts, always attempt to utilize powerful phrases. Simply attempting something is not motivation; rather, it is attempting to perfect it. So, if you can think clearly and forcefully, you can succeed.

## 10.Broaden Your View:

When the amygdale produces fear and other unpleasant feelings, your mental viewpoint immediately becomes focused on watching for and avoiding the danger. You thus fail to consider the good parts of your life or original solutions to the issue. Is there a way to see the source of your stress as a challenge or a chance for progress instead? This may assist you in refocusing your mental energy and brain chemicals toward controlling the stressful circumstance, which can actually increase your motivation and efficiency.

## 11. Utilize psychological triggers to keep your heart and mind in harmony.

Balance is something you make, not something you discover. January Kingsford

The majority of the time, this occurs when your heart and intellect get impasse. While the brain uses logical reasoning, the heart is emotionally connected. However, in order to act, you must maintain a balance between the two, which is only attainable by applying a psychological trigger.

Think about a situation when your intellect is telling you not to set a timetable but your heart is telling you to. So, instead of giving up in such a circumstance, think the opposite. Consider how much less stressed you will be if you are aware of your whole day's agenda and everything will be finished on time. This method will bring your mind and heart into harmony and inspire you to go on.

## Choose the Right Attitude:

Focus in what you can learn from the circumstance and the abilities and talents you have to handle it rather than trying to avoid stress. Making avoidance your main objective will make it harder for you to locate solutions or support. Instead, consider proactive, constructive methods to cope with the stressor and how handling it could help you learn and develop.

**What are the five methods for reducing stress?**

To manage stress and lessen the general tension of daily tasks, try the following five suggestions:

1. Make use of guided meditation.
2. Learn to breathe deeply.
3. Maintain a healthy diet and workout routine.
4. Organize your time on social media.
5. Relate to others.

**The stress pandemic**

Stress Research Month, which takes place in April, seeks to educate people about the effects of the stress epidemic and constructive strategies to deal with stress. Today, occupational stress is an issue that affects every country. According to a Gallup poll, 80% of American employees experience some kind of work-related stress. And half admit they need assistance figuring out how to cope with it. While certain levels of work-related stress are common, excessive or ongoing demands may cause whiplash, which has a detrimental effect on people's health and limits their capacity to operate. According to studies, smoking, inactivity, and chronic job stress are all detrimental to one's physical and mental well-being. Long-term work stress puts your defenses on high alert and increases your chances of type 2 diabetes, high blood pressure, chronic pain, and a weakened immune system.

**What are the top 5 symptoms of stress?**

When under stress, you could experience:

irritable, furious, impatient, or tense.

overloaded or overburdened.

anxious, uneasy, or terrified.

It's as though your mind is racing and you can't relax.

being unable to relax.

Depressed.

lifeless and uninterested.

like you've forgotten how to laugh.

## What does an economic downturn mean?

Economies that are sluggish may have low GDP growth or high unemployment. Although slow economies are often seen to be negative for the majority of businesses, there are chances for certain companies and sectors. Quantitative easing is a strategy that central banks may use to jolt a stagnant economy.

## How can I stop feeling so stressed out?

You may start to breathe more deeply, encourage greater stability, and experience a sense of self-control returning.

Orient to what is happening now, start the grounding process, start naming your bodily sensations, slow down, and start noticing what feels good.

## Why am I experiencing such stress at home?

Numerous factors, like a loud atmosphere, a disgruntled spouse, financial concerns, or even menial household chores like doing the washing machine or mowing the yard, all contribute to homegrown stress. It's important to take stress seriously.

## Here are 4 approaches of handling life's difficulties that don't entail hitting your head with a wall.

1.  Take a deep breath.
2.  Plan ahead and think of solutions.

3. Third tip: Change your perspective.
4. Own your stress.

## How can I recognize the telltale indications of stress?

- Being angry, annoyed, or cranky easily.
- Feeling overpowered, as if you need to take charge or that you are losing control.
- Having trouble unwinding and calming your thoughts. Feeling unloved, unimportant, and dejected as well as having poor self-esteem.

## Symptoms of Excessive Stress

- chest discomfort, fast heartbeat
- nausea, vertigo
- constipation or diarrhea
- using drink or drugs to unwind and "de-stress"
- eating excessively or insufficiently
- putting off or skipping over obligations
- enduring constant worry
- I'm feeling overpowered
- Inability to focus
- racing or tense thoughts
- agitation and a difficulty to unwind
- irritability and depression

## Does Stress Really Have the Power to Make You Sick?

Stress, regrettably, is an unavoidable part of life. Given that the corona virus has become a part of our everyday life, you could feel more anxious than ever. However, can stress really make you ill?

Yes, to quickly respond.

The following health issues may be made worse by stress sickness:

Anxiety.

poor sleep.

Irritability.

not being able to concentrate.

you have trouble finishing your task.

drug and alcohol abuse problems.

poor dietary choices.

Dr. Adam Borland, a psychiatrist, says that a little stress might help you stay alert. According to Dr. Borland, "handling a manageable degree of stress and anxiety aids in preparing us to face the challenges of daily living."

Additionally, contemplating a challenging problem could help you come up with a solution. Thinking about an argument with your spouse while "in your head" may actually help you see the situation from a fresh perspective.

Dr. Borland asserts that worry only becomes a problem when it starts to limit your ability to accomplish the things you need or want to do. Naturally, if worry starts keeping you up at night or makes you resort to food or alcohol as a kind of self-medication, it might be harmful to your health.

## The part cortical plays

The sympathetic nervous system of the body becomes active during periods of physical or mental stress, according to Dr. Borland.

This causes what is known as the fight-or-flight reaction, in which your body gets ready to either physically protect itself against a danger or flee.

You could detect immediate physiological responses like:

- elevated heartbeat.
- breaths quickly.
- respiration difficulty.
- Dizziness.
- Headache.
- Nausea.
- tension in the muscles.

## What signs of cardiac stress are there?

Symptoms and Signs

(Often abrupt and severe) chest pain

respiration difficulty.

irregular or fast pulse.

Sweating.

Dizziness.

## Can stress put a load on your heart?

Heart disease and stress

Constant stress may already put your heart under a lot of pressure. Blood pressure goes up with stress. Your body becomes more inflammatory under stress. Your blood might become more triglyceride and cholesterol-rich under stress.

**Can stress sometimes be good? False or true?**

Your body's response to a demand or difficulty is stress. Stress may sometimes be advantageous, such as when it keeps you safe or helps you reach a deadline. However, stress that lasts a long period may be harmful to your health.